GREAT WESTERN PICTORIAL

No.3

THE TONY STERNDALE COLLECTION

COMMISSIONED BY
SUE STERNDALE

© Wild Swan Publications Ltd. and Sue Sterndale 2006

ISBN 1 905184 11 5

Designed by Paul Karau
Printed by Amadeus Press, Cleckheaton

Published by

WILD SWAN PUBLICATIONS LTD.

1-3 Hagbourne Road, Didcot, Oxon, OX11 8DP

A pannier tank propelling a number of engines alongside 'A' shop at Swindon around August 1948. The 'Bulldog' on the left of the group was perhaps one of the fifteen or so engines of the class that were stored or condemned during that summer. The next engine, Canton's ex-Barry 'B1' class 0–6–2T No. 238, had been condemned in June, though still retained much of its pre-grouping character. To its right ex-TaffVale 'O4' class 0–6–2T No. 200, had been renumbered in December 1946 from its first GWR number, 300; this engine was condemned in July 1948. Swindon shed's own ex-Barry Port locomotive, No. 2195 (BP & GV No. 5, named *Cwm Mawr* until 1939), was far from withdrawal, surviving until 1953. Taunton 'Castle' No. 5077 *Fairy Battle*, on the right was recorded as undergoing an Intermediate repair at Swindon during August and September.

INTRODUCTION

Tony Sterndale had two consuming interests – steam railway locomotives and photography. So it is not surprising that he spent the first part of his working life as a professional railway engineer and the second part in the photographic business. Nor is it surprising that he should have combined his two interests by taking many thousands of fine photographs of railway subjects, mostly steam locomotives, from his teens until his seventies. This period coincided with the decline of the steam locomotive; so Tony's legacy of photographs forms a poignant record of the passing of the great days of steam on the railways.

In temperament, Tony was ebullient, with a ready wit and a puckish sense of humour, He was also no respecter of persons and was always ready to 'cock a snook' at authority and deflate the pompous.

This album of a selection of his best photographic work is published as a tribute to the scale and quality of his achievement, and to his lifelong spirit of enterprise.

Tony's life history was an intriguing one. He was born Anthony Craufuird Sterndale in London in 1924. His New Zealand-born father served in the British forces in both World Wars, and worked in the interwar years as a manager in the Imperial Bank of India. So Tony spent part of his childhood in India, enjoying the privileges of a young sahib in the Raj.

His schooling was at Ryford Hall and Wycliffe College, and it was during this period that he first showed a natural talent for the graphic arts, winning the coveted silver medal of the Royal Drawing Society in 1934. At the same time he developed a keen interest in railways, and in 1941 he joined the Great Western Railway as a 17-year-old apprentice, signing five-year indentures to train in 'fitting, turning and erecting' work at Swindon Works. One stipulation was that he had to attend night classes for mathematics and design before qualifying as an engineer. His training at Swindon included some rather basic tasks, such as cleaning out locomotive boilers, but he was later transferred to operational duties, and finally promoted to the drawing office, on locomotive test work. By this time he was already known about Swindon as the 'man with the camera'; he took his very compact secondhand Leica III B camera everywhere, and used his entrée to the vast Swindon Works and other railway premises to take photographs of steam locomotives in the workshops, on shed, in service on the line, and from the cab.

Tony left the railway in the early 1950s to work briefly as a draughtsman in Esso Petroleum's London

'850' class 0–6–0ST No. 2007 at Worcester in the summer of 1949, one of the two remaining ex-Great Western saddle tanks outside the docks and works complexes on the Western Region. The No. 6 pilot engine board signified work 'Round the back' of London Yard from 3.30 to 11.30 p.m., although the engine was also commonly used on the No.1 afternoon turn to the coal drops, and over the Vinegar branch. No. 2007 was withdrawn from Worcester in December 1949.

1

In a late summer's evening c.1952, a 'Hall' is pictured on an up milk train at Oxley Sidings, comprising half-a-dozen tanks and a passenger brake, with its class 'C' lamps penetrating the gloom. This was probably the 8.5 p.m. Dorrington to Marylebone train, due through Oxley around 9.30 p.m. This service, which commenced operations in 1936, ran to the Rossmore Road premises of the old Independent Milk Supply Company, immediately to the north of the ex-Great Central Railway's London terminus. Oxley engine shed was off the left-hand edge of this photograph, in the middle distance.

Old Oak's '47XX' class 2–8–0 No. 4705 leaving Oxley Sidings to join the Up Main with a class 'D' vacuum freight, probably the 8.10 p.m. Oxley to Paddington. An '84XX' 0–6–0PT is seen waiting to the left on the Up Goods Loop with a freight, with a second service behind it. There were two dozen sidings on the up side at Oxley, divided into 'Old', 'Middle' and 'New' Yards; the 'Old' Yard handled mostly traffic for the West Midlands, whilst the 'New' was reserved largely for through main–line traffic. Goods services came largely from the main Birkenhead line and the busy Crewe branch (via Wellington).

A Bath Road 'Castle' approaching the junction at Wootton Bassett with the 8.20 a.m. Weston-super-Mare to Paddington in 1952. This train ran non-stop from Bath to Paddington, and was due at Wootton Bassett Junction around 9.50 a.m., with some 90 minutes still to run. The photograph was taken from the footplate of '47XX' class 2–8–0 No. 4704 which was being held on the down main. The Badminton cut-off route to Bristol and South Wales is seen diverging to the right underneath the A420 road bridge – the same road may be seen crossing over the main line at the tail end of the express. Wootton Bassett West signal box roof is visible beyond the 'Castle'.

headquarters. But he soon returned to the railways, albeit with the London Underground at its Acton Works in West London, where he spent eleven years as a designer-draughtsman and research assistant. Typical of his work there was a soul-destroying investigation into sliding door failures.

It was at this time that he made the acquaintance of Sue Richardson, who worked in Lewis Newcombe's in Old Bond Street, where he bought his film, paper and other materials for his own developing and printing of his photographs. They were married in Marylebone in 1959, and five years later they took the big decision to leave London with their two children and set up a photographic business in the lively Hampshire town of Lymington, where his family owned property. Five years later Tony took over a rival business in a better position in the town and renamed it the Camera Shop. With her own photographic knowledge, Sue was able to play her part in this successful enterprise, and she also accompanied Tony on many of his jaunts round the country and abroad to photograph steam locomotives – by then a dying breed. For one trip to Czechoslovakia, Tony drove the revolutionary Citroen 'Traction Avant' car which his grandfather had purchased new before the war. In 1972

Tony bought his prized orange-coloured MG-B, which he drove (like Jehu!) all over the country until 1987, often with Sue as 'co-pilot'. For much of his earlier photographic work, Tony was able to use his father's equipment, which had been stored during the war and included a Zeiss Nettel Press camera. Later cameras included an Olympus OM2, a Nikon FM2, a Leica M3 and a Bronica S2A, together with many other models (both new and secondhand) which were being 'tested' for the shop.

In 1993, Tony and Sue decided to sell the business and retire. Referring to his intention of cataloguing his thousands of photographs, Tony told a local reporter "I am faced with such a huge backlog of work, and life goes so quickly. I really must get some into print". Sadly, it was not to be. Soon after his retirement came the onset of illness. After some months in hospital, he died rather tragically, of Alzheimer's disease, in 1998.

Looking at the totality of Tony's railway photographic work, there are some features which stand out. For one thing, the great majority of the photos are black-and-white. He produced a substantial number of colour slides of good quality, but he delighted in developing his own photos and much preferred monochrome. Secondly, he

'Bulldog' 4-4-0 No. 3406 *Calcutta* with parcels stock alongside platform No. 1 at Bristol Temple Meads in 1948, probably soon after completion of her 'General' repair in February of that year. The engine moved back to Pontypool Road after her repair but was recorded as 'stored' at Swindon from July 1948; following storage, she subsequently went to Hereford shed, and was withdrawn in January 1951. Beyond, one of the final Lot (358, of 1946/7) of 'Counties' is seen in platform No. 2 with another down stock train, carrying 'D' lamps. A number of parcels train arrivals in the down direction used No. 1 platform.

had access at Swindon to many (some very old) official negatives of steam locomotives, and his output included prints produced from them. With these and his own negatives, he tried out a variety of developing materials until he achieved the perfect print. Another feature of his work was its range, which was not confined to GWR subjects, but extended to all the other main-line railways and, indeed, to Ireland and several Continental systems. He also had an eye for the rare and unusual, including minor and preserved lines, industrial railways, and breakdowns.

As may be imagined, Tony had, over sixty years, acquired a massive archive of railway material – thousands of his own photos in negative or print form, hundreds of prints from old official railway photographs, hundreds of books on locomotives, boxes full of technical locomotive drawings, locomotive number plates, railway paintings (including some of his own) and even a large 3½ in gauge model locomotive.

Since Tony's death in 1998, a large part of this collection has been disposed of, including prints, books, drawings, paintings, locomotive plates and some photographs. All of this material has 'found a good home' with such recipients as the Great Western Museum in Swindon. It is hoped that the rest of the Sterndale archive, including particularly thousands of film negatives, will end up where they can be worked on and consulted.

This album is a selection of Tony's photos of Great Western locos, largely at Swindon Works and others he sought on visits to South Wales. Many of the prints had been carefully marked with photographic details, such as the camera used and the chemicals employed – but (infuriatingly!) no details of subject, date or place. Fortunately, the locomotives can be fairly easily identified, and there are a number of pointers to the approximate dates.

In closing this tribute to Tony Sterndale and his work, we quote two anecdotes which give an idea of his sometimes mischievous spirit and his ability to debunk.

The first story is from the time when Tony was a research assistant at London Transport's Acton Works. Organisations like LT are constantly being asked to send technical staff on courses. Busy departments cast around to see whom they can spare to send. Tony had a roving commission and no specific duties, and so was the ideal candidate to go on courses. Eventually he could claim that he had been sent on more courses than anyone else in London Transport. At last the worm turned. Tony was sent on an expensive three-week course at Melton Mowbray. After the first week, he wrote to Acton saying that the course was a complete waste of his time and LT's money, and that he was returning to London forthwith and would report back to Acton on the next Monday morning. The letter was not addressed to his immediate boss, but to the Chief Mechanical Engineer in person. One suspects that the reaction of the Acton hierarchy may have had something to do with Tony's decision to 'go it alone' and set up shop in Lymington!

A driver's eye view of the junction at Risca on 20th July 1952, looking north-westwards with the signal box in the divergence of the two routes. The '42XX' class 2–8–0T seen ahead with a train of hopper wagons was passing from the Up Relief line onto the Western Valleys route, cutting across the front of the '72XX' containing the photographer. The latter engine, standing on the Up Main, was awaiting its passage before taking the Sirhowy line, possibly en route to Aberdare.

The other tale concerns a ride which Tony took on the footplate of the 'Royal Scot' from Euston to Glasgow. Looking very dirty and crumpled after many hours on a greasy, rocking locomotive, Tony made his way to the station hotel to book a room for the night. The sanctimonious Scottish receptionist took one look at Tony's scruffy attire and told him firmly that there were no vacant rooms in the hotel. Undeterred, Tony went outside to the nearest telephone box and phoned the hotel. Using his best 'public school' voice (which was natural to him, but could be accentuated when necessary), he asked authoritatively for a room for the night, and was given a booking. Upon which he returned to the reception desk to claim his booking, to the consternation of the self-important receptionist!

It is no wonder that Tony Sterndale was known everywhere as a 'character'. To the railway fraternity, he will also be long remembered as a fine chronicler of the last decades of the steam locomotive.

P.E.G.

Sue Sterndale would like to record her thanks to Paul Garbutt for writing the introduction, John Copsey for researching and writing the captions, and Alan Wild for supervising the photographic prints and keeping an eye on the project.

An Old Oak 'Hall' passing the familiar office block on the approach to Swindon Junction station with the 3.55 am. Fishguard Harbour to Paddington train (No. 711) c.1951. This was the daily (Mondays excepted) connection from the Waterford and/or Rosslare steamers, seen running here non-stop between Newport and Reading, where it called to set down only. Another steamer, from Cork, was served by the following 4.55 a.m. Fishguard. At this time, the Old Oak 'Hall' was scheduled to work outwards with the 6.55 p.m. Paddington (or a Relief portion) the previous evening, and is seen here returning from Cardiff with the boat train.

The Bristol & Exeter company had eight Pearson broad-gauge 4–2–4T locomotives, built in 1853/4 with 9ft driving wheels. These were replaced or renewed from 1868/73 by a similar design with flangeless 8ft 10 in drivers; here, a pair of the latter wheels is seen in the concentration yard ('C' shop, handling of scrap) at the west end of the Swindon factory site during the 1950s.

'Duke' class 4–4–0 No. 9064 *Trevithick* reversing along the engine line outside 'A' Shop, Swindon Works, in 1948. No. 9064 was a Gloucester engine at this time, and was used mostly on pilot or local freight turns; she was recorded on the morning Gloucester to Honeybourne freight in February 1948, and in the following year, the Oxford to Slough, Bordesley to Banbury and Gloucester to Hereford local freights.

0–6–2T No. 242 (ex-Barry Railway 'B1' class No. 44) outside 'A' (Erecting) Shop, Swindon Works in 1948. The engine had been condemned in January 1946, but was temporarily taken into stock again at Swindon during April 1947 and used as a works shunter. She was finally condemned in November 1947. During the Second World War, No. 242 was recorded on goods trains between Barry and Bridgend.

Ex-Brecon & Merthyr Railway 0–6–2T No. 504 (B & M No. 39) from Newport (Pill) shed photographed outside 'A' Shop, Swindon Works in January 1948, the month of her withdrawal from traffic. Built by R. Stephenson & Co. in 1910, this engine was one of a class of four (extended to eight in 1914) utilised on mineral traffic. By 1948, the engine was fitted with an ex–Rhymney Railway Belpaire boiler with top feed, and a Great Western smokebox and chimney.

0–6–2T No. 504 (ex-Brecon & Merthyr Railway No.39), seen again at Swindon Works in January 1948. On 13th March 1946, she was recorded on the 10.15 am. Newport (West Mendalgief) to Rhymney Valley (via Maesycwmmer) train, Target N7, with a load of 43 empties; this was typical of the work of those six of the class allocated to Pill shed around this time.

'Metro' class 2–4–0T No. 3561 seen in the Concentration Yard at the west end of the factory site in January 1948. She moved from Bristol to Swindon in September 1946, and was utilised for local and factory duties. Having been built in January 1894, No. 3561 was the oldest 2–4–0T in service, being withdrawn in October 1949. Notice the sandbox fitted on the boiler, forward of the tank.

0–6–0T No. 6 (ex–Weston, Clevedon & Portishead Railway) seen on the engine reception roads at Swindon on 30th January 1948. The independent WC&P Railway was closed in May 1940, and two of its locomotives were taken into GWR stock (as Nos. 5 and 6); No. 6 was the former London, Brighton & South Coast Railway 'Terrier' No. 53 *Ashtead*, sold by the Southern Railway (No. 643) to the WC&P in 1937. Stationed at St. Philip's Marsh, both engines were periodically loaned out during the war, and No. 6 went to Ilkeston. The engine was condemned in January 1948.

A lengthy class 'K' freight behind an 'Aberdare' on the Up Goods loop opposite Rodbourne Lane box, Swindon, in 1948. At the beginning of that year, a dozen of the class were still extant, though by July the number had been reduced to four, the last of which went in October 1949. The engine reception shed is seen to the right of the engine.

No. 9083 *Comet*, pictured outside the weigh table house at Swindon Works – just off the south-western corner of 'A' Shop – in February 1948. The engine underwent a 'General' repair in January and February of 1948, after which she returned to Winchester for use on the Didcot, Newbury & Southampton line services. This engine survived until December 1950, though with long periods of storage from July 1948.

Kitson 0–6–2T No. 410 (ex-Taff Vale 'O3' class No.18) seen outside the CME's office block at the south-eastern edge of the Loco Works on 31st March 1948, shortly after withdrawal. This engine had been rebuilt with Great Western-style tanks, cab and bunker, although it retained a boiler of the 'O3' design. No. 410 had arrived from Cardiff Canton, where it latterly carried out work as shed pilot.

Another member of the 'O3' class, 0–6–2T No. 411 (ex-Taff Vale No. 19), seen at Swindon Works in March 1948. No. 411 had its original bunker rebuilt in the GWR style, but otherwise remained mostly in its original form. As with No. 410, she is seen with a rebuilt 'O3' boiler. The engine was withdrawn from Cardiff in February 1948.

A view of the inside motion of No. 411, March 1948.

4–4–0 'Bulldog' No. 3421, seen in the Concentration Yard at Swindon on 27th April 1948, having been condemned a few days earlier; she did not long survive the torch. This was one of the eighteen 'Bulldogs' built in 1906 that never carried a name, as opposed to numerous others that had names removed to avoid 'confusion' or duplication. She had been a Swindon engine since 1935, working much of the time on the M & SWJ line, including allocations to Andover Jct. Following a visit to the Works in 1944, she appeared in a black livery.

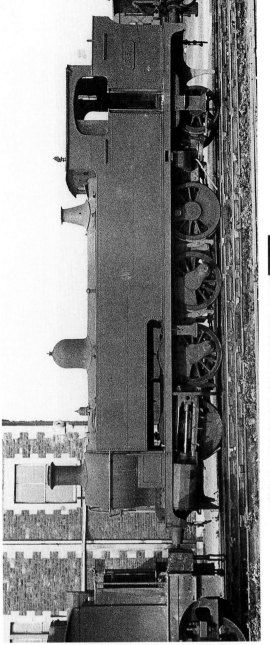

The 0-8-2 wheel arrangement was not indigenous to the Great Western, although the company effectively acquired five such tank engines to stock as it took over the working of the Port Talbot Railway in 1908. Of these, two had been obtained by the PTR from the Cooke Locomotive Company of the USA in 1900, and three more from Sharp, Stewart in 1902. Seven very similar designs were also acquired by amalgamation with the Barry Railway in the grouping of 1922. The PTR engines were utilised on the mineral trains from the Llynvi and Garw Valleys, based at Duffryn Yard, but by 1936 only No. 1358 survived, and was used on shunting duties. Here, No. 1358 (ex-PTR No.17) is seen outside the CME's Offices at Swindon Works in March 1948, having been withdrawn from traffic a month earlier. Shedded latterly at Danygraig, she was used on such turns as the Swansea Docks Hump Yard Pilot.

A Down express at Swindon in February 1948 behind a 'Castle', believed to be Old Oak's No. 5023 *Brecon Castle*, with a 4,000-gallon Hawksworth tender attached. This view was taken from outside the Carriage Paint Shop, with the chimneys of the wagon works smithy in the background.

'1901' ('850') class 0–6–0PT No. 1993 in green livery with a 'W' suffix painted underneath the numberplate, standing in the turntable yard at Swindon Works on 8th March 1948, after a 'General' repair. No. 1993 would shortly make her way back to Barry shed (the Cardiff Valleys 'CVBRY' already painted on the footplate frame, at the front), where she would remain until withdrawal in April 1951.

Chalford's '14XX' class No. 1441 at Swindon in 1948, again a plain green livery with the 'W' suffix under the numberplate. The 'lion and wheel' emblem would appear experimentally around July 1948, though not generally on tank engines until the middle of the following year. No. 1441 would soon be back on the Stonehouse or Gloucester auto-trains from Chalford.

'44XX' class 2-6-2T No. 4408 in the Turntable Yard at Swindon Works in March 1948 following a 'General' repair, but before other unspecified adjustments were made; she was out of traffic at Tondu for over three months on this occasion. Along with No. 4404, this engine was used on the Tondu and Porthcawl branch freights around this time. Other engines of the class were to be seen on mixed traffic duties on the Much Wenlock, Princetown, Ashburton and Exeter (City Basin) branches. The 4ft 1½ in diameter driving wheels were the smallest size for engines in general traffic, and comparison with the pony wheels serves to emphasise this.

Bath Road 'County' No. 1014 *County of Glamorgan* in the Swindon Works Turntable Yard in March 1948, after an 'Intermediate' repair. Following her return to Bristol, in good mechanical condition, she was frequently recorded on the shed's London turns. The legend 'British Railways' had been applied to the tender, as it was to a number of tank engines in the Works at this time.

No. 5042 *Winchester Castle* taking the curve between the Loco and Wagon sections of Swindon Works on the Gloucester line as she approached Swindon Junction station with an up Cheltenham Express, early in 1948. The engine was stationed at Gloucester, and is probably seen here with the 11.30 a.m. Cheltenham service, a scheduled twelve-coach train (with dining car) that would return as the 6.35 p.m. Paddington.

A view of Swindon Drawing Office, 1948. Tony Sterndale worked here for a while on locomotive testing projects.

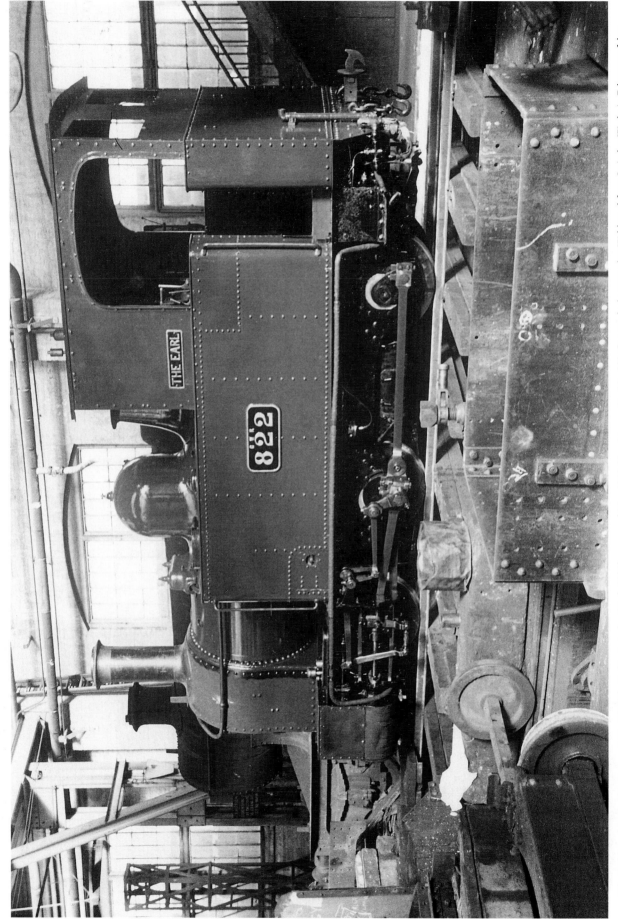

The Welshpool & Llanfair Railway's No. 822 *The Earl* in Swindon Works 'A' Shop, around May 1948. Her sister engine No. 823 *Countess* had returned to Welshpool from Swindon Works in February of that year after a 'General' repair, releasing No. 822 to visit the Works for similar attention. *The Earl* returned to Welshpool in June. At this time, there was one daily weekday return trip (Wednesdays and Saturdays excepted) between Welshpool and Llanfair Caereinon, and occasionally a second on Mondays, conveying such loads as slag for agricultural purposes, and livestock traffic. By 1950, the services had increased to a regular daily trip, with an additional run when required.

An inside-cylinder casting for an ex-Southern 'West Country' class 4–6–2, seen in the 'A' Shed Machine Shop, Swindon Works, early 1948 – an early benefit of nationalisation.

'O' Shop, Swindon Works, in 1948. This was the tool room, situated on the western side of the main Loco Works complex, alongside the Turntable Yard.

The 'A' Erecting Shop at Swindon Works, showing the west side of the main electric traverser in 1948. The pit roads were slightly raised to provide access to the traverser unit. A diesel electric engine of the '15101' class can be seen on the near right, probably the first in the batch of six on order.

Assembling an 0-6-0 diesel-electric shunter at the 'A' Erecting Shop, Swindon Works, 1948. A wheel set for the locomotive can be seen on the right, marked '502', which was the original number of No. 15101. The frames, wheels and other mechanical parts were built at Swindon, whilst the engines, motors and other electrical fittings were supplied by contractors English Electric.

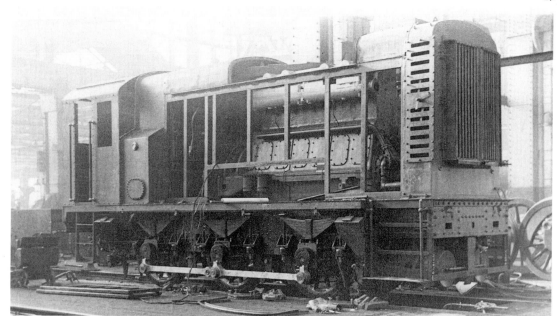

The diesel in an almost-complete condition, with wheels and coupling rods.

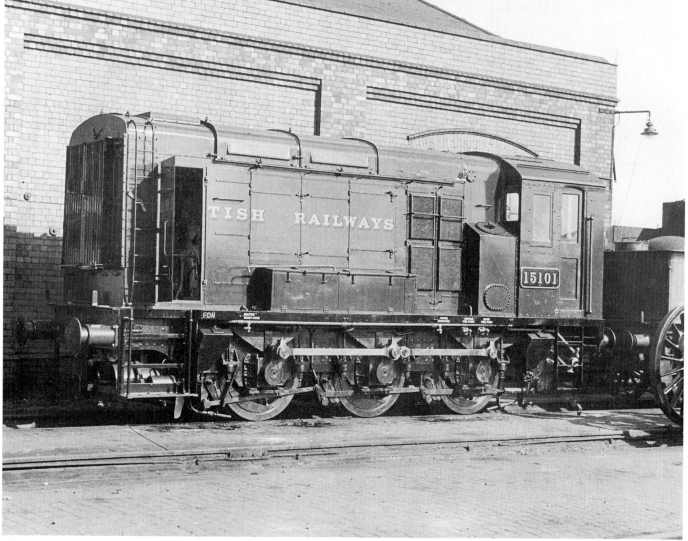

No. 15101, complete with GWR-style numberplate, outside 'The Barn' in May 1948. This loco went to Old Oak Common, where it replaced the ex-GWR diesel-electric No. 2 (renumbered 15100 in March), then at work in Acton Yard. On completion of the order, all six were allocated to Old Oak (along with No. 15100).

In these three views, No. 5010 *Restormel Castle* is seen at Swindon shed in June 1948, resplendent in the new experimental light green livery with red, cream and grey lining. She was attached to Hawksworth tender No. 4008 (Lot A182) after the overhaul – on which lettering was in plain white – and the pair remained together for two years. The background to the name and numberplates was also initially light green, but this was soon changed to black. In all, nine 'Castles' were turned out in this livery. Although carrying the Canton code, the engine was soon transferred to Landore after this 'General' repair, and continued to be a common sight at Paddington.

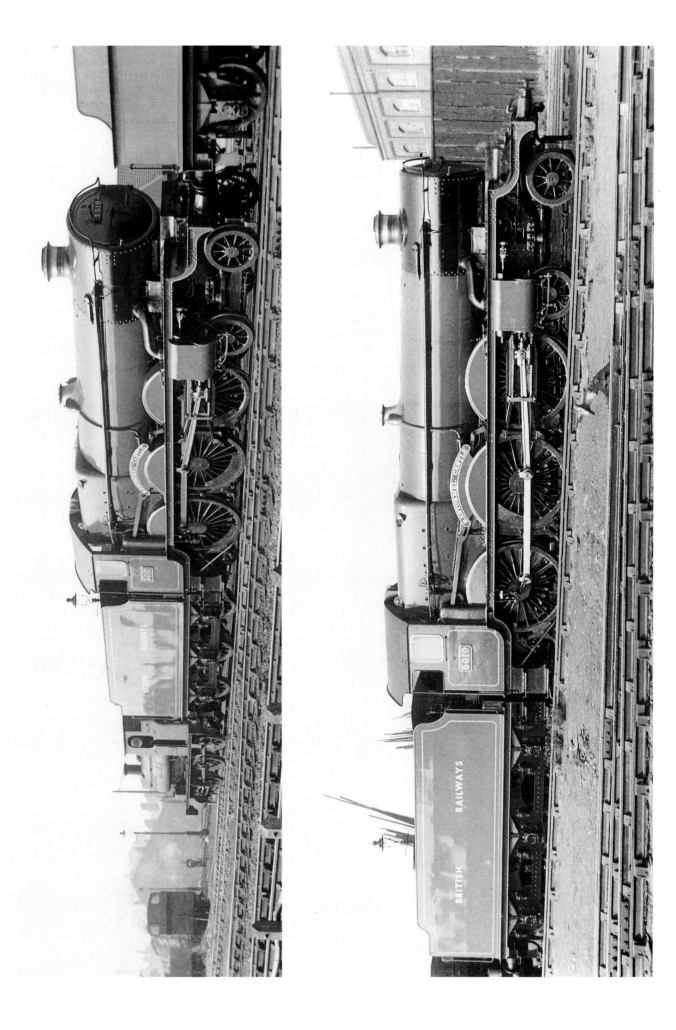

Ebbw Junction's 'Hall' 4–6–0 No. 4941 *Llangedwyn Hall* at the entrance to Swindon shed, April 1948. The number had been painted on the front bufferbeam in the traditional manner, as only the experimental-liveried engines appear initially to have carried the smokebox numberplates. However, it was not long before nearly all engines did. The Gloucester main lines are seen in the foreground in this view.

'Star' No. 4026 (*King Richard* until 1927, then *Japanese Monarch* until 1941), now with 'Star Class' painted on the centre driving wheel splasher, is seen outside the Iron Foundry, alongside the Bristol main line, at Swindon Loco Works in 1948. The shaded letters on the tender were utilised on the standard green livery engines. No. 4026 was transferred to Taunton in July 1934, and would remain until withdrawal in February 1950. The Taunton code (TN) can be seen on the footplate frame.

The Great Western constructed two 8-wheel tenders: No. 1755 (the *Great Bear's* 3,500-gallon, double-bogie tender, Lot A76) in February 1908, and No. 2586 (4,000 gallons, Lot A123) in July 1931. The experimental tender No. 2586 was initially coupled with No. 5919 *Worsley Hall*, though only until September 1931, when it was paired briefly with No. 4091 *Dudley Castle*, then with No. 5001 *Llandovery Castle*, until August 1936. During the war years, it ran with No. 5071 *Spitfire* (to March 1942) and 5049 *Earl of Plymouth* (to April 1944). Here, the tender was attached to No. 5068 *Beverston Castle*, pictured at the Works Turntable Yard, Swindon, in April 1948.

'Hall' No. 6910 *Gossington Hall* at Swindon shed in June 1948, with the General Stores building in the background. A new smokebox numberplate had been fitted, though the shed allocation was still painted in the 1940s Great Western manner, on the footplate frame behind the buffer beam, showing the traditional 'PDN' for Paddington (Old Oak Common). She is seen here in a new, lined black livery, with plain lettering on her tender; shortly afterwards, the lettering was replaced by the new 'lion and wheel' emblem. On 27th June 1946, No. 6910 had been derailed at nearby Wootton Bassett whilst working the 11.50 p.m. Paddington to Carmarthen vacuum freight, though she was back at work some six weeks later.

'King' class 4–6–0 No. 6001 *King Edward VII* at Swindon Works Turntable Yard during June 1948 in the experimental blue livery. The experimentally-liveried engines carried a brass smokebox numberplate at this time, although the accompanying shed plates did not appear until the latter part of 1949; again the traditional 'PDN' can be seen on the footplate framing. Draughtsman Freddy Yates is seen on the footplate.

Another 'King' to carry the experimental blue livery was Laira's No. 6025 *King Henry III*, seen on Swindon shed in July 1948. No. 6025 had been an Old Oak engine since its entry into traffic during August 1930, and was transferred to Plymouth on completion of the 'Light' repair in July 1948. The change of shed altered its working life a little, as it no longer found itself occasionally on Old Oak's daily Paddington & Wolverhampton turns (except when being 'borrowed' by that shed), but remained on the West Country services. The engine retained its blue paintwork until January 1954.

Old Oak 'Castle' No. 5023 *Brecon Castle* in the light green livery outside 'A' Shop' at Swindon Works in June 1948. No. 5023 was recorded regularly on Bristol and Weston trains out of Paddington during 1948/9, with occasional forays to Weymouth, Plymouth, Cardiff and Wolverhampton. The 'lion and wheel' emblem can be seen on the tender side, with a large rectangle for the legend 'British Railways', the lettering carried out initially by hand.

'King' No. 6009 *King Charles II* on the Swindon Works 'triangle' in July 1948. The engine is seen in the experimental blue livery, with the new 'lion and wheel' emblem on the tender. No. 6009 saw a very long-lived allocation to Old Oak shed, over her entire working life from April 1928 to September 1962, during which period she amassed almost two million miles.

Old Oak 'Hall' No. 6910 *Gossington Hall* outside 'A' Shop at Swindon Works, July 1948, now with the 'lion and wheel' emblem in place of the former painted title 'British Railways'.

No. 6910 *Gossington Hall*, seen around the same time on Swindon Works 'triangle'. In addition to vacuum freight turns, No. 6910 was recorded on fast and semi-fast passenger duties to Weymouth, Plymouth, Bristol, Oxford, Wolverhampton and Bicester during 1948/9.

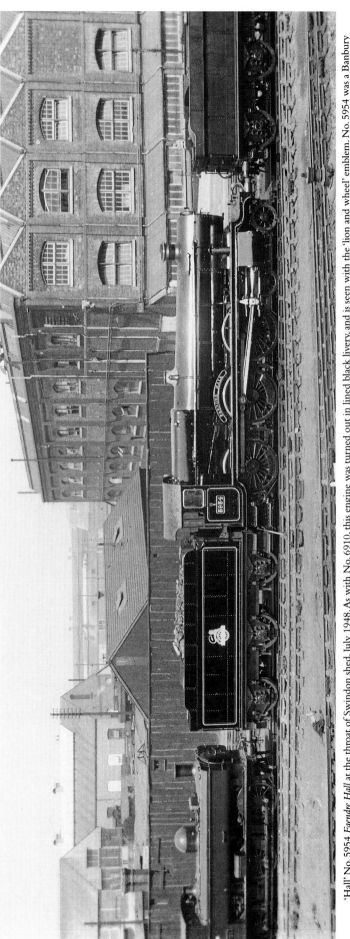

'Hall' No. 5954 *Faendre Hall* at the throat of Swindon shed, July 1948. As with No. 6910, this engine was turned out in lined black livery, and is seen with the 'lion and wheel' emblem. No. 5954 was a Banbury engine, and spent most of her time on freight turns, though with the occasional passenger duty (probably more so when ex-shops). Behind the engine, and to the left of the General Stores building, can be seen the Mason's Yard ('D2' Shop) beyond the fence, with the ends of the Timber Store, and Carpenters' Shop ('D1') in the middle distance.

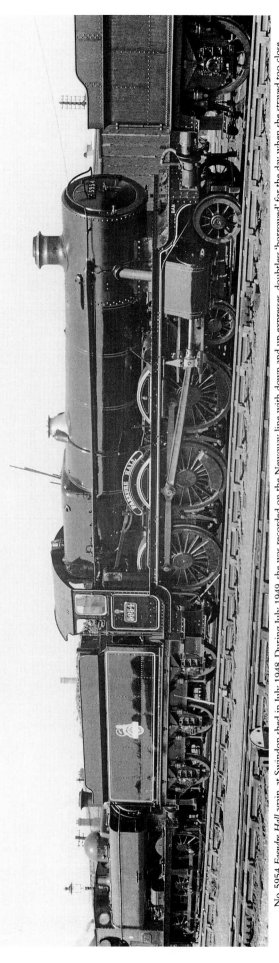

No. 5954 *Faendre Hall* again, at Swindon shed in July 1948. During July 1949, she was recorded on the Newquay line with down and up expresses, doubtless 'borrowed' for the day when she strayed too close to Laira shed. The pannier tank coupled behind is believed to have been Tyseley's No. 5701, in contrasting green livery, though without any ownership markings.

No. 5023 *Brecon Castle* in light green livery on Swindon shed during July 1948. With repairs completed, the engine may have been on its way back to Paddington and its home shed, Old Oak. During the latter half of 1948, she was regularly seen on the Saturday 1.50 p.m. Bristol to Paddington duty, believed to be the return engine working of the 9.5 a.m. Paddington to Bristol at that time.

The first run of the 'plum and spilt milk' livery stock on the 9.5 a.m. Paddington to Bristol took place in mid-August 1948, and here the train is seen passing through the station and alongside the carriage shops behind a 'Castle'. It ran non-stop to Bristol, slipping a three-coach portion at Bath.

The return run of the 'plum and spilt milk' stock was as the 4.15 p.m. Bristol to Paddington train. This service had called at Bath, and would slip at Reading. The slip portion at the rear comprised a Slip coach (No. 7070 specified) and a pair of Corridor Brake Composites, which worked to Bath on the 9.5 a.m. Paddington, then by the 12.30 p.m. local from Bath (11.55 Chippenham) to Temple Meads. Following the slip at Reading from the return service, the trio worked to Paddington on the 7.52 p.m. Weymouth express). The tail lamps on the last vehicle were for the only (or the last) slip portion, this being a red and a white lamp in the horizontal plane; second and third slip portions carried different combinations or positions of red and white lamps.

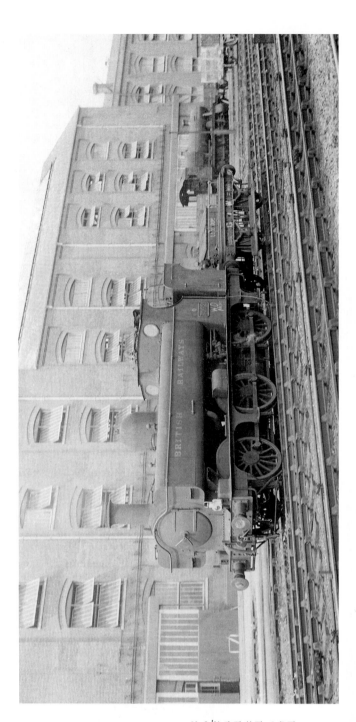

Swindon '1501' class 0–6–0PT No. 1542 outside 'A' Shop (Erecting) with a Loco Department shunting truck in the autumn of 1948. The 'British Railways' lettering across the tank was applied during a visit to Stafford Road that summer. On completion of that repair, No. 1542 was recorded as being used on a morning Tipton to Dudley freight, operated by a Stafford Road crew. In the postwar era, this engine had often been used as the Works 'Field Pilot' at Swindon.

At the beginning of 1948, there were three of the ten '3571' class 0–4–2Ts still in traffic. In March, No. 3575 was transferred from Severn Tunnel Jct. to Swindon, and is seen here shunting at Swindon Carriage Works in August 1948. This engine was also used on the Highworth branch. No.3575 was withdrawn in October 1949, the penultimate survivor of the class, whilst the last went in December of that year.

Ex-Burry Port & Gwendraeth Railway 0–6–0ST No. 2195 (formerly *Cwm Mawr*) derailed on pointwork at Swindon Wagon Works in July 1948. These pictures show the rear of the engine being raised by means of jacks, the front end having already been supported on blocks to enable a move across onto the rails. Whilst most of the Burry Port engines were still being used for freight duties or dock pilots in their home territory, a few were working elsewhere on pilot or trip turns, as with Swindon's No. 2195.

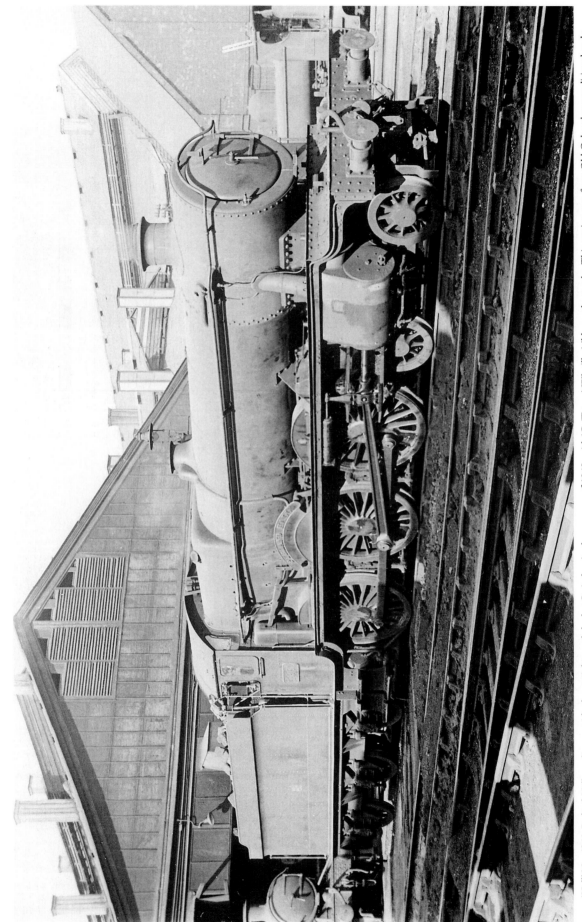

'Hall' No. 4961 *Pyrland Hall* standing outside the straight-road shed at Swindon in the summer of 1948, with 'G (Totem) W' still visible on the tender. This engine was from Old Oak, whose traditional code 'PDN' can be seen on the footplate valance, below the outside steampipe. During 1948, No. 4961 was recorded on the 10.45 a.m. and 2.15 p.m. Paddington to Cheltenham services, both of which brought her to Swindon.

No. 6325 from Southall shed with an up goods train on the Gloucester line, passing Swindon shed in 1948. This was a class 'F' train, and may well have been the overnight 11.10 pm. (or 1.35 am. on Mondays) from Oxley Sidings, due into the transfer sidings at 9.41 a.m., and rostered for a 'D' or 'E' class engine. A panoramic view of the shed can be seen behind the coal stage, with the straight-road building to its left, and the roundhouse to its right.

Swindon's oil-burning '43XX' No. 6320 pictured outside the roundhouse shed at Swindon in 1948, alongside the refuelling point for oil-burning locomotives. This engine was modified for oil firing in March 1947, and was converted back to coal burning in August 1949. During this period, she was recorded on goods trains, but also on passenger duties with the 1.50 p.m. Swindon to Didcot and the 4.38 p.m. Didcot to Reading, returning with the 7.0 p.m. Reading to Swindon; this was formerly a 'Bulldog' turn.

The height of the coal stage at Swindon is accentuated in this view of the yard in 1948, looking south, from inside the straight-road shed.

Stourbridge Jct. '51XX' class 2–6–2T No. 5134 is seen at Swindon shed in 1948. At this time, Stourbridge housed around 25 of the class, predominantly for local passenger duties on the Wolverhampton, Worcester, Birmingham, Stratford and Leamington lines, although No. 5134 was recorded on the No. 18 pilot – one of the banker targets which spent much of its time on the Old Hill line – in October 1948. They were also utilised on local freight turns to such destinations as Bordesley or Cannock Rd.

No. 3575 at Swindon shed, September 1948, still with her 'STJ' shed code on the footplate valance. She was withdrawn in October 1949.

'Duke' No.9083 (ex-3283) *Comet* in Swindon's roundhouse shed, summer 1948. This engine had been at Didcot since May 1938, and much of her work had been on the Didcot, Newbury & Southampton line, though she was also utilised on some of the less-exacting goods duties to the London area, and passenger duties to Reading. Latterly, No. 9083 had also been shedded at Winchester for the morning goods.

A collection of 4–6–0s around the turntable inside Swindon shed in 1948, including an Old Oak 'Castle' on the left. Swindon's allocation at this time included a selection of 'Star' and 'Saint' classes as well as 'Halls'.

'3571' class 0–4–2T No. 3575 inside Swindon shed during the summer of 1948. This engine had been allocated to Severn Tunnel Jct. since December 1941, though with occasional spells at Pontypool Road, and it appears that she was much used for steam heating of stock and other shed duties. No. 3575 moved to Swindon in February 1948 for light duties around the factory and shed, but also work on the Highworth branch.

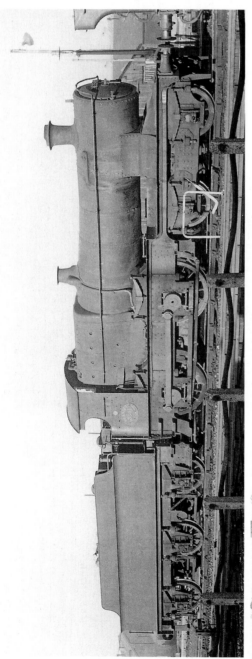

'Bulldog' No. 3341 *Blasius* at Swindon shed, probably during late 1949. An Exeter engine by this time, No. 3341 was utilised mostly on station pilot duties at St. David's station. She was fitted with a smokebox numberplate in late 1948 – which may be seen in this view – and was withdrawn from traffic in November 1949.

Swindon's '850' class 0-6-0PT No. 2014 at Swindon shed, summer 1948. No. 2014 had been gravitating around the Bristol Division since 1927, primarily at Swindon and Bristol, though she also worked on the Kemble & Cirencester branch before and during the war. She had been withdrawn prior to the war, but was reinstated. Her later duties at Swindon included the carriage shop pilot, and Highworth branch turns. She was 'converted' into an 0-4-2T c.1942 by the removal of her trailing coupling rods.

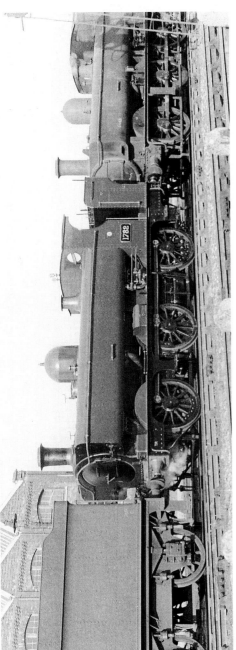

A newly-painted '655' class 0-6-0PT No. 1782 at Swindon shed during August 1948 on completion of a General repair that had involved a boiler change, and had seen her out of traffic for 95 days. No. 1782 had moved to Truro in May 1942, and would run back there within a few days of this photograph to continue her work on local shunting duties, with perhaps the odd freight turn down the Falmouth line.

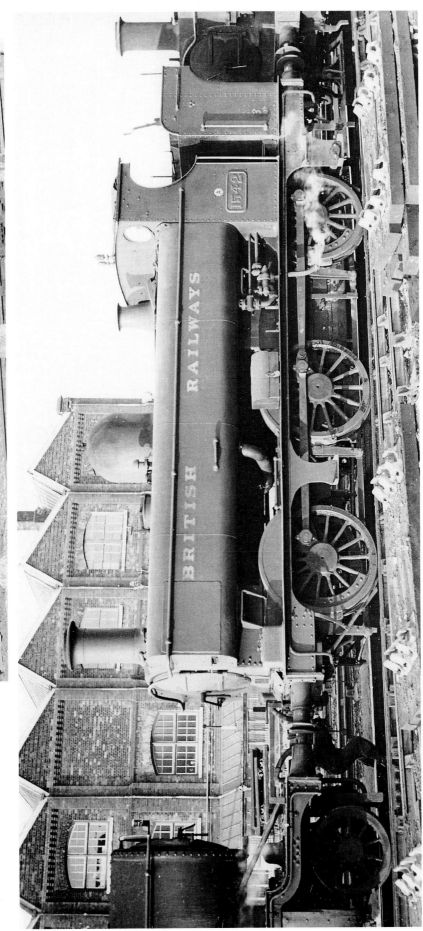

'645' class 0-6-0PT No. 1542 on the Ash Road at Swindon shed, 1948. Amongst her recorded duties at Swindon was that of Field Pilot, though sister engines elsewhere were still being used on local and branch goods turns.

Nos. 78624 and 79244 with tenders painted for the LMS at the stock shed, Swindon Works, during 1948. Both had just returned from interchange trials on the Southern Region, for which these new tenders were attached. The two engines would soon be placed back into the storage sidings out at Marston Crossing, a couple of miles to the east of Swindon, where they remained unattended for some time; they were not part of the batch operating on the Great Western or Western Region, but on the system for storage.

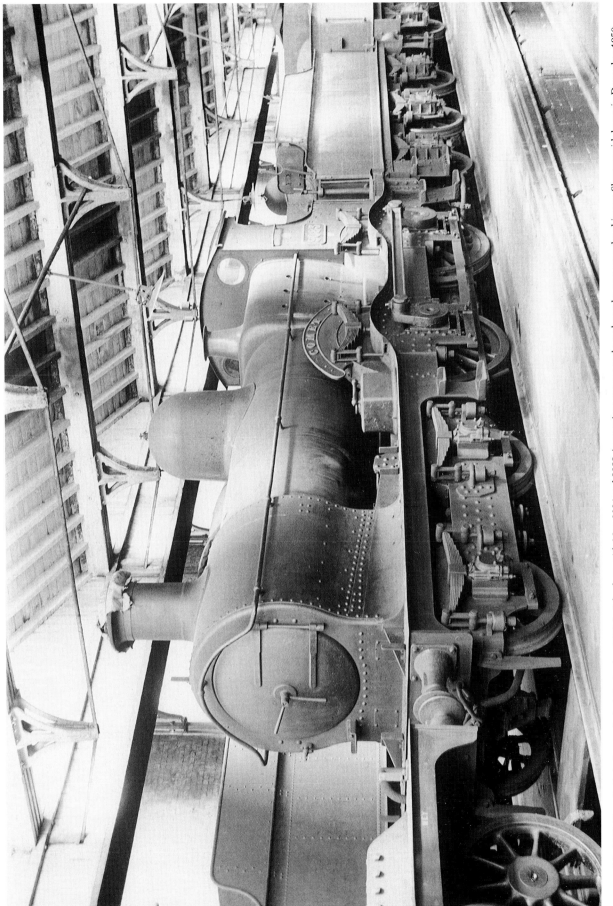

No. 9083 *Comet* in Swindon stock shed, September 1948. In July, along with Nos. 9084 and 9089, it went into storage, and a sack can be seen over the chimney. She was withdrawn in December 1950.

A 'WD' 2–8–0 on a down class 'E' goods on a trials run passing the Carriage Shops at Swindon Works, with the LNER dynamometer car attached. In these trials, Cardiff's 'WD' 2–8–0 No. 77000 was recorded as the engine in use, following a light repair in April/May 1948. She went to Old Oak shed in July.

Scottish WD 2-10-0s were also involved in the trials, with No. 73774, 73781, 73794 and 73795 transferred onto the Southern and Western Regions. Here, No. 73774 (from Motherwell shed) is seen passing the Carriage Stock Shed on the approach to Swindon with an up coal train in late August 1948, again with the dynamometer car behind the tender.

No. 73744 with the ex-LNER dynamometer car outside Swindon Works, 1948, with the spire of St. Mark's beyond the front of the engine. The roof fittings of Rodbourne Lane box can be seen above the car.

LMS 2-8-0 No. 48189 on a down trials goods with the ex-LNER dynamometer car, passing the Carriage Shops at Swindon Works. The engine came from Hellifield shed, West Yorkshire, and was seen alongside a '28XX' (No. 3803), Eastern Region 'O1' 2-8-0 No. 63789, 'WD' 2-8-0 No. 77000 and the 2-10-0s.

In contrast to foreign engines and dynamometer car, No. 5098 *Clifford Castle* is seen with the indigenous Swindon dynamometer car on trials at Newport station with a down express, c. 1948. This car was built in 1901, and remained in use until replaced by a Hawksworth vehicle in 1961.

An interior view of the dynamometer car, showing various controls and recording equipment, including a Hallade recorder. A retractable, flangeless wheel was located underneath the car for speed measurement. The car's operating section was located centrally, with saloon sections containing a table and bench seating at each end. Observation windows were provided at both ends, with an armchair in each external corner, whilst a shallow, central lookout section was built into the sides. The lavatory compartment was located behind the two seated operators. The man seated at the table was Sam Ell with, it is believed, an AM shop fitter alongside him.

KEEP AWAY FROM THE MAN AT THE CONTROLS

The Swindon Test Plant control desk, seen with the operator at the desk. The man on the left is believed to have been either Stan Davies or Phil Perry. The test plant was located in the south-east corner of 'A' shop, near to the works' turntable yard, and was used to test locomotives at various speeds up to 80 mph., ascertaining such information as drawbar pull, water and fuel consumption. The plant could be utilised by engines ex-works, or for comparative tests of aspects requiring a stable, identical trial environment. It was introduced around 1903.

Right: No. 5087 *Tintern Abbey* on the test plant, Swindon Works. Having been brought to the plant on a traverser, the engine was moved onto the table of the machine, standing on its wheel flanges. Once the machine's wheels had been adjusted for the engine's configuration, the table would be lowered until the engine's wheels were resting on those of the machine; this permitted the engine's wheels to rotate during the test.

Didcot '2301' No. 2579 on the Test Plant, December 1949, taking part in comparative tests with an LMR 'Class 2' locomotive. The water supply for the engine was obtained from the two tanks on the platform, from which consumption was measured. The figure (wearing a beret) on the platform was Ernie Nutty, with, it is believed, Stan Davies behind him.

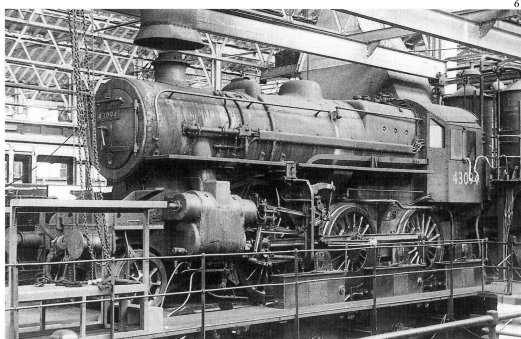

Ex-LMS 'Class 4F' (later '4MT') 2–6–0 No. 43094 on the Test Plant in the late 1940s. It was probably here for comparative tests, and was 'equivalent' to the '43XXs' and 'Prairie' tank classes.

Worcester 'Manor' No. 7818 *Granville Manor* on the Test Plant in May 1952, with a temporary chimney fitted for test purposes. At the rear, an adjustable firing platform was provided to accommodate any height of cab footplate, with a coal bunker and weighing machines adjacent. Ernie Nutty is seen standing at the rear of the cab, observing the test, with an AM shop fitter at rail level.

Swindon 'Hall' No. 4905 *Barton Hall* with a 3,500-gallon tender on a down evening local leaving Swindon for Bristol in 1948. The engine was attached to this tender in October 1947, but it proved to be an eventful partnership, for the engine was known to have been 'stopped' on three occasions in 1948 for attention to the tender. The train was probably the 5.0 p.m. Swindon to Bristol, via Chippenham, which was formed Van Third, Third, Compo, Third and Van Third, corridor stock; this was one of four such sets running four-day cycles, operating a dozen services between stations within the Reading and Weston-super-Mare area.

A 'Star', believed to be Bath Road's No. 4033 *Queen Victoria*, on a down conditional (run when required) relief train for Swansea in the summer of 1948. This train, which left Paddington at 3.45 p.m., was the first part of the 3.55 p.m. Paddington to Fishguard Harbour, and was due to pass Swindon at 5.13 p.m. running non-stop Paddington to Newport, calling thence at Cardiff, Port Talbot and Neath en route to High Street station. Eight coaches were scheduled, though there were nine on this occasion. On peak summer Fridays and Saturdays, the 3.45 p.m. would run through to Fishguard conveying ten coaches, with a further three at the rear for Cardiff.

Oxley shed's 'Hall' No. 4944 Middleton Hall on a lengthy down class 'H' goods at Rushey Platt in 1948, passing beneath the M & SWJ line bridge. The train may have been the 12.55 p.m. Banbury to Stoke Gifford, which two surviving records show to have been worked by a Reading 'Hall' and a Banbury 'WD' 2–8–0 locomotive around this time.

No. 7818 *Granville Manor* on the ex-M & SWJ line near Swindon Town station in 1948. At this time, Cheltenham shed also had No. 7815, and the two engines were to be found on the 10.5 a.m. Cheltenham to Southampton passenger, returning with the 4.30 p.m. Southampton passenger, and the 1.55 p.m. Cheltenham to Southampton passenger, returning with the 7.9 p.m. Southampton freight.

No. 426 (formerly No. 888; ex–Brecon & Merthyr No. 41) at Newport Pill on 17th May 1947, with a row of pannier tanks behind her. Brecon & Merthyr workings by this time were mostly handled by 0–6–0PTs, but No. 888 (426) was still utilised on coal traffic along the traditional Rhymney Valley routes. Renumbered as 426 on 19th April 1947, she was shedded at Pill, but with short allocations out at Llantrisant, and was withdrawn in March 1950. She had been rebuilt at Caerphilly with a standard taper boiler (No. 2) in 1941.

At a time when the Brecon & Merthyr's finances were buoyant with an increase in coal traffic, the company ordered four 0–6–2Ts from Stephenson & Co. (Nos. 36–39), very similar in design to the class 'R' engines of the Rhymney, appearing in traffic during 1909/10. A second batch of four very similar engines (Nos. 40–43), again from Stephenson, were introduced in 1914. Here, No. 425 is seen at Newport Pill in 1947; an engine of the second batch, she was originally No. 40, renumbered 698 at grouping, and 425 on 6th June 1947. She was withdrawn in March 1951.

Canton 'Castle' No. 4083 *Abbotsbury Castle* on the 8.15 a.m. Neyland to Paddington, leaving Port Talbot on 1st May 1948, with the towering bulks of Mynydd Dinas and Mynydd Emroch forming the backdrop. The scheduled formation of this train was for five coaches from Swansea (including the dining car, third in the formation) at the head, five from Neyland, and three from Pembroke Dock at the rear.

Ex-Taff Vale '04' class 0–6–2T No. 296 (formerly TV No. 94) at Port Talbot in 1948. This class was designed for mixed traffic working, and comprised four batches of locomotives from different manufacturers, including Manning Wardle in the case of No. 94 (296) in 1907. Although it received a number of Great Western fittings (including bunker), it was one of five engines (of the 41) that was never rebuilt with a GWR standard boiler. A Duffryn Yard engine in the postwar era, she was mostly involved in shunting turns, and was officially recorded on the Duffryn No.8 Pilot (Glenhafod Colliery; Port Talbot Docks & Copperworks Jct.) duty in July 1945, and as the Port Talbot Docks Trip engine in July 1947.

Another of the Stephenson 0–6–2Ts built for the Brecon & Merthyr Railway, No. 428 (B & M No. 43, then GWR No. 1113 from the grouping) was recorded at Margam on 1st May 1948, after receiving her second Great Western number on 16th October 1947. A Newport Pill engine for many years, No. 428 was transferred to Duffryn Yard in December 1947 to provide additional engine power during and following the development works in the area, which included the new steelworks. These developments would culminate with the massive marshalling yards at Margam, opened in 1960.

Cardiff East Dock shed was part of the Cardiff Valleys Division of the CME's Department, built under the 1929 Act in the very centre of the dock and industrial complex, and opened in 1931 on the site of part of the former Rhymney (Cardiff Dock) shed. It housed many ex-Rhymney and TaffVale Railway 0–6–2T engines for goods and shunting work, and a large stud of GWR and constituent 0–6–0 tanks for shunting duties. Here, Nos. 2754, 2124 and 155 are pictured at Cardiff East Dock shed on 1st May 1948. The pannier tanks were of the '2721' and '2021' classes respectively, and both had been transferred across from Canton during 1942.

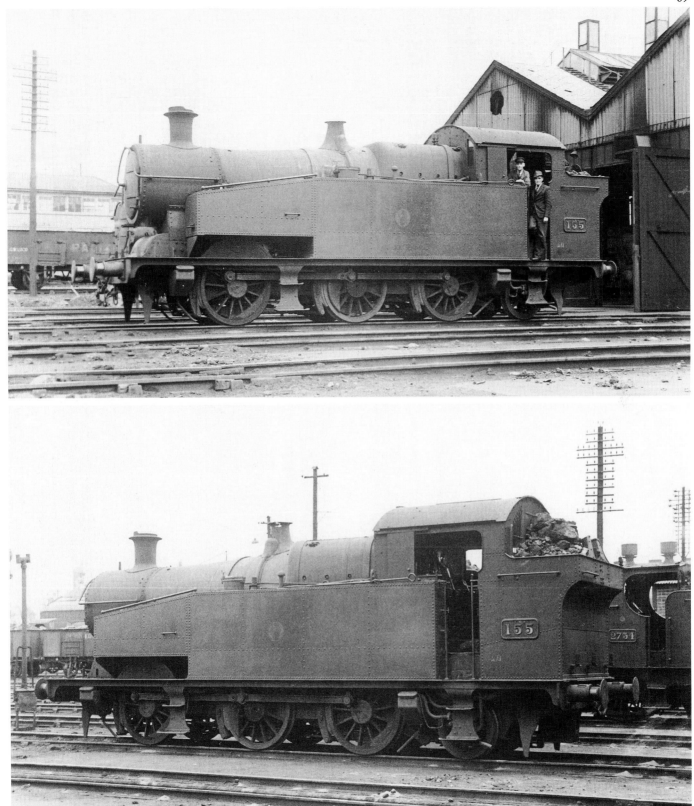

In 1908, Kitson delivered three large 0–6–2Ts to the Cardiff Railway, numbered 33 to 35, these being more powerful than any of that wheel configuration that Kitson had provided to the Cardiff company before. At grouping, these three engines were renumbered 153–5 respectively, but the first two were condemned or sold in the mid-1930s. Here, No. 155 is seen at Cardiff East Dock shed on 1st May 1948, showing its large 2,260-gallon side tanks – more capacious than the Great Western 2–6–2T, 0–6–2T or 2–8–0T classes, and only 200 gallons or so less than the '72XXs'. This engine had been rebuilt at Caerphilly with a No. 3 taper boiler, together with a Great Western cab and bunker, and as such survived until September 1953. One of its known workings was on the 'D5' freight from Roath Basin Jct. to Whitchurch.

Ex-Rhymney Railway 'M' class 0–6–2T No. 33 in Cardiff East Dock shed, April 1948. This engine was No. 16 when introduced into traffic, along with five others, during the summer of 1904, and in late GWR days they were utilised for shunting or short-distance pilot trips. Only one of the class received a standard Great Western boiler, whilst the others retained Rhymney designs until the end, although some fittings were changed. No.16 was withdrawn in March 1951.

The most common design absorbed into the Great Western at the grouping was the 0–6–2T, of which some 420 were taken into operational stock, but around 160 engines of the 0–6–0 tank configuration were also acquired. Former Cardiff Railway 0–6–0T No. 684 is seen here at Cardiff East Dock shed on 1st May 1948, one of a class of four saddle tanks delivered by Hudswell, Clarke in 1920, and then numbered 32. The engine was rebuilt with a standard No. 11 boiler, pannier tanks and other standard fittings in 1936, and was utilised on the many shunting turns and trips out of Cardiff East Dock. She was withdrawn in May 1954.

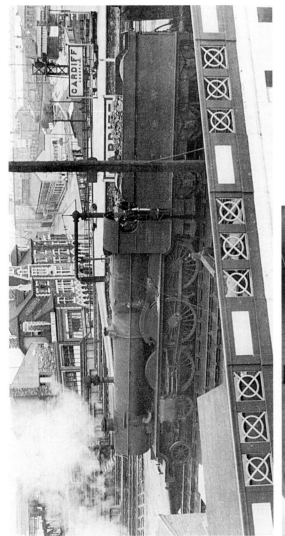

Bath Road 'Star' No. 4033 *Queen Victoria* on an up local train, probably for Bristol, at the east end of Cardiff General in 1948. The prominent station boards display the 'General' suffix, introduced in 1922 to identify it from the other stations in the city acquired at the grouping. In the background, the line from the adjacent Riverside station to Clarence Road may be seen.

Cardiff Queen Street station on Sunday, 15th August 1948, with No. 5681 and a sister engine at the head of the 8.50 a.m. to Rhymney. No. 5681 was from Cathays shed, and is seen carrying that shed's passenger target 'CB'. The '56XX' in the train shed was waiting with a second service, probably the 8.20 a.m. ex-Penarth to Merthyr, also due to depart at 8.50 a.m.

Ex-Taff Vale 'O4' class 0-6-2T No. 280 outside the coal stage at Cardiff Canton shed in the late 1940s. This was formerly No. 6 of the TVR, and entered traffic in July 1908. This engine was at Barry in the early postwar era, moving to Ferndale in July 1946; at the latter, she was recorded on the 'FP4' Pilot, shunting Porth and Tynewydd yards, with a goods trip to Trealaw. No. 280 returned to Barry in October 1946, and was transferred to Canton in September 1947. Here, she was officially recorded on the No. 18 Pilot at Newtown Goods on 19th February 1948, working the Long Dyke Mileage and shed transfer duties. She survived until May 1949.

The former Rhymney Railway 'R' class 0-6-2T No. 42 (RR No. 46) from Radyr shed with the 'Y27' goods on the Relief line to the east of Cardiff General station in May 1948. This duty started with the 4.20 p.m. from Radyr Jct. to Pontypridd (Northern Jct.), then continued with the 6.35 p.m. from Pontypridd (via Radyr, Penarth Curve East and the main line) to Newtown Goods, as seen here. The engine returned from Newtown with the 10.20 p.m. for Radyr Jct. by the same route. On Saturdays, this service ran some three hours earlier. On the left, the 'Taff' lines are seen climbing away prior to crossing over the mains to gain access to Queen Street station and the Valley lines.

Barry shed in 1948, showing '850' class 0–6–0PT No. 1993, ex-Barry Railway class 'E' 0–6–0T No. 783 (BR No. 50), and what may have been Taff Vale class 'A' 0–6–2T No. 440 (TVR No. 52), all of which were allocated to the shed. The small 'E' class engine was built by Hudswell, Clarke in 1890 for light work in restricted locations, and Barry classes 'B' and 'B1' (0–6–2T), 'E' and 'F' (0–6–0T) were the only ones allowed over the extensive Syndicate Sidings (No. 1 Dock). Further, the 'E' class alone was permitted along the line leading to the West Breakwater; this was a curious line, where access to the breakwater was by a removable section of rail laid over the pier branch, just to the west of Barry Pier station.

Ex-Barry class 'B' 0–6–2T No. 213 shunting at Barry in 1948. Along with their 'B1' counterparts, these engines worked primarily on the Barry main-line coal traffic between the Rhondda, Taff and Rhymney valleys and Cadoxton, but in later years the 'B' class was more confined to shunting duties. This engine had been withdrawn in the summer of 1939, but was reinstated later that year due to the wartime situation. It was finally withdrawn in January 1949.

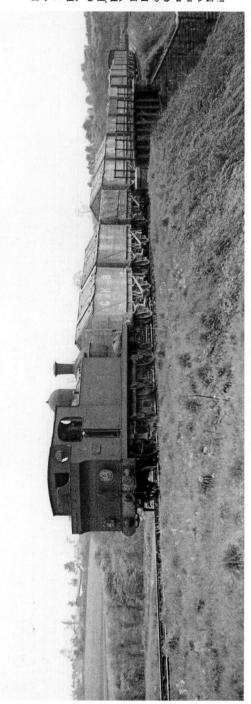

Barry Railway 'B1' class 0-6-2T No. 240 with the 'Y10' goods train at Llandaff in early 1948. The engine was allocated to Radyr in postwar years, and was often recorded on the 'Y10' Pilot in that period; this commenced at 6.50 a.m., ran the 11.30 a.m. Radyr Quarry Jct. to Creigiau Quarries empties; the 1.25 p.m. Creigiau Quarries to Cardiff, Dowlais Works (East Moors) stone, via Queen St. North; and the 4.0 p.m. Dowlais Works to Radyr Quarry Jct. freight. Another round trip of empties and stone between Radyr and Creigiau was carried out in the evening, if required, leaving Quarry Jct. at 7.15 p.m. The main trip was recorded on 19th January 1948 with No. 240, Driver J. Drew and Fireman W. Nunn on the footplate, and Guard D. Roach in the van, all from Radyr.

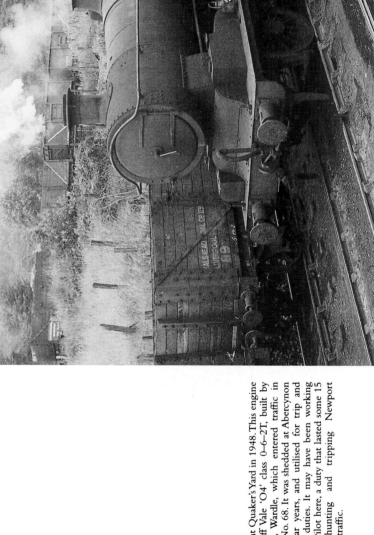

No. 295 at Quaker's Yard in 1948. This engine was a Taff Vale 'O4' class 0-6-2T, built by Manning, Wardle, which entered traffic in 1907 as No. 68. It was shedded at Abercynon in postwar years, and utilised for trip and shunting duties. It may have been working the JP4 Pilot here, a duty that lasted some 15 hours, shunting and tripping Newport Division traffic.

Another ex-Taff Vale '04', No. 283, on the T13 mineral at Treorchy in 1948. This had been a Treherbert engine since April of that year, and was working the Treherbert to Cadoxton train which ran under the direction of the Cardiff Controller. For this duty, the engine left shed at 12.57 p.m. for the van sidings, then at 1.5 p.m. with the van for her train. The route taken was most probably via Trehafod Jct. and the Barry line to Cadoxton.

Treherbert ex-TaffVale 'A' class 0–6–2T No. 365 (TVR No. 130) on a mineral train near Treorchy in 1948. This class was used extensively on passenger work, but records indicate that the eight 'A' engines at Treherbert were also frequently used on goods and pilot duties, as seen here. No. 365 was recorded on the T20 pilot, an evening trip to Stormstown Jct. (Abercynon), on 8th November 1948.

In 1884, Kitson delivered three 0-6-0 tank engines (Nos. 141-3) to the Taff Vale company for work over the 1¾-mile Pwllyrhebog Incline (serving the Clydach Vale branch). The engine propelled the empties up the inclines – which commenced with a stretch of 1 in 13, and eased out to 1 in 30 – the weight of the empties being counterbalanced by the weight of loaded wagons descending on adjacent trackwork. The loaded portion was connected to the engine by a substantial wire rope which ran via a drum at the top of the incline, and passed under the train of empties. At the grouping, the engines' numbers were changed to 792-4, and again in 1948/9 to 193-5. The duties in 1948 required two engines at Pwllyrhebog working targets PH1 and PH2, both starting at 8.0 a.m. for an 8-hour day; this involved working on the incline, shunting at the top and bottom, and trips to the Clydach Vale Colliery. The third engine was usually spare at Treherbert. No. 193 is seen here on a freight in the district during 1948.

Bath Road 'Castle' No. 4084 *Aberystwyth Castle* passing Swindon Works 'A' shop at the head of a down stopping train, with an LMS coach leading, during early 1949. Rodbourne Lane box can be seen on the right-hand edge of the photograph, partly shrouded by No. 4084's exhaust. The '30XX' class (ROD) 2–8–0s in the background were being scrapped.

'Metro' 2-4-0T No. 3561 at Rodbourne Lane – the box was just off the left-hand edge of the picture – with one of the timber sheds in the background. The photograph was taken from outside the 'A' (Boiler) Shop, looking south.

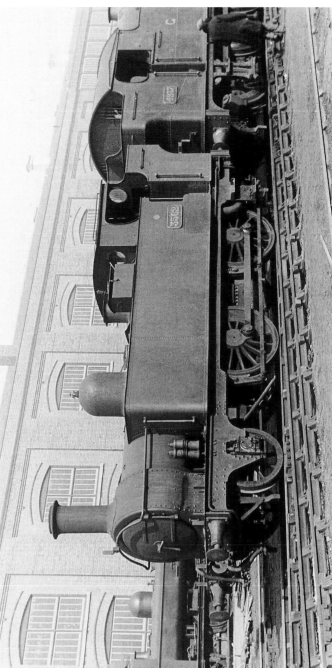

Oxford 'Metro' No. 3562 outside Swindon Works, with Newport (Pill) '42XX' 2-8-0T No. 4237 alongside, in early 1949. The 'Metro' was taken out of traffic in February 1949, and was cut up two months later. Aberdare '57XX' No. 3655 is seen in the background.

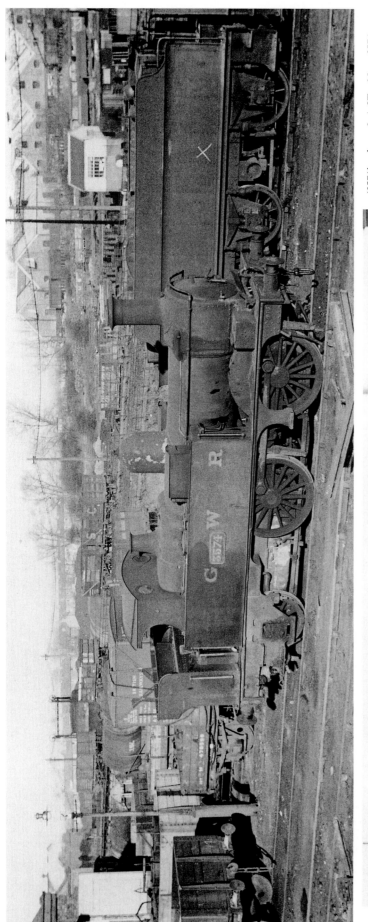

'3571' class 0–4–2T No. 3574 pictured outside Swindon Stock Shed, alongside the Gloucester line, Autumn 1949. She was the last of her class when withdrawn in December 1949. The buildings in the distance housed the Carriage Paint and Body Repairs Shop, the northernmost element of the Carriage & Wagon complex located to the north of the station.

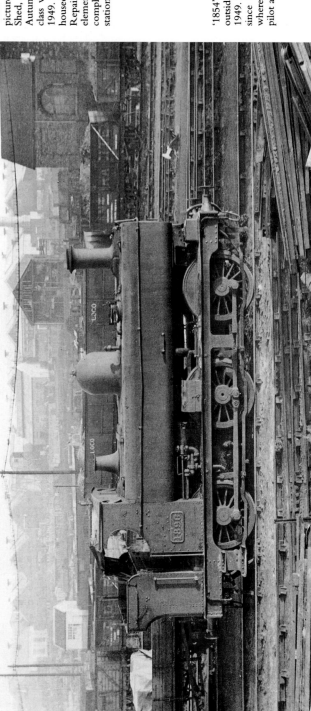

'1854' class 0–6–0PT No. 1896 outside Swindon Stock Shed, Autumn 1949. This had been a Welsh engine since 1923, latterly at Newport Pill, where it had been used mostly on pilot and shunting duties.

0–4–2T No. 3575 standing outside the end of the CME's office block at Swindon Works, 1948. The GWR roundel can just me made out above the numberplate on the side tank.

'Metro' No. 3561 was parked next to No. 3575, unofficially named 'The Flying Maggot'. This engine saw many changes over the years: built in 1894, she originally had an open cab and condensing gear for working on the underground lines. She also had a 820-gallon tank, but this was changed for a longer, 1,080-gallon type in December 1898. At the same time, she was also given a replacement sandbox on top of the boiler, behind the chimney, which is evident here, and was unique amongst the 'Metros' in this respect. The cab and an enlarged bunker were most probably added during the interwar period.

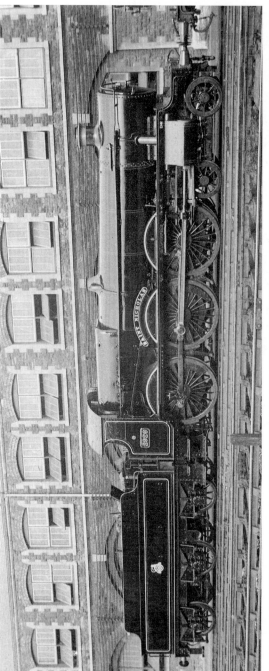

Chester's 'Saint' class 4-6-0 No. 2926 *Saint Nicholas* visited Swindon Works during September and October 1949 for a Heavy General repair, followed by a repaint. She had earlier experienced persistent trouble with a cracked frame over the leading coupled wheel on the left-hand side, the fourth time this had happened in that area, but the problem had now been put right. No.2926 is seen in this view with her all-black lined livery, carrying the smaller BR emblem that was utilised on lined 3,500-gallon tenders due to the restricted space.

No. 7800 *Torquay Manor* outside Swindon Works weigh table house in 1951. Underframe and smokebox show signs of attention, but the other portions of the engine do not. Still a Banbury engine, No. 7800 was at Swindon Works for a 'Heavy Intermediate' repair from 9th April to 3rd May of that year.

In October 1949, the first of the '16XX' class 0–6–0PTs emerged from Swindon Works, effectively replacements for the small, but very useful '2021' class engines. No. 1600 was allocated to Barry, and carries the GWR-style code on its footplate valance, together with the Cardiff Valleys ('CV') prefix. As may be seen, it was carrying a smokebox numberplate, but no insignia.

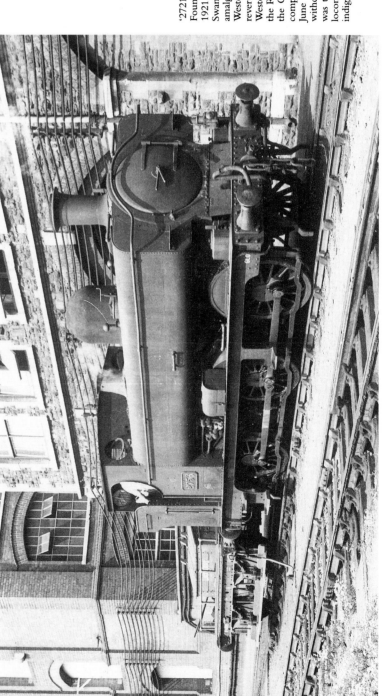

'2721' class No. 2756 outside Swindon Works Foundry in June 1949. For a short time in late 1921, this engine became Rhondda & Swansea Bay No. 33, but following amalgamation of that company into the Great Western on 1st January 1922, quickly reverted to its original number. Ten Great Western locomotives had been transferred to the R & SB over the years from 1907, when the GWR took over the operations of that company. No. 2756 went to Gloucester in June 1938, to Swindon in 1949, and was withdrawn from use shortly after this picture was taken. No. 2756 was the last 'R & SB' locomotive to be withdrawn, though the last indigenous engine went in April 1940.

No. 46 (ex-Rhymney Railway 'R' class No. 97) at Swindon Concentration Yard during 1949. These engines, with 4ft 6in driving wheels, were designed for heavy mineral traffic. Stationed at Radyr from June 1946, No. 46 was recorded on the 7.45 p.m. Radyr to Severn Tunnel Jct. mineral in December 1946, and on the 11.0 a.m. Little Mill Jct. to Landore freight in January 1947. She was withdrawn from traffic in July 1950.

Ex-Taff Vale 'O4' class 0–6–2T No. 298 in Swindon Concentration Yard, 1948. A Ferndale engine for most of the postwar era, she was recorded on several Maerdy & Porth passenger duties during 1946, working on such turns alongside 'O4' and GWR '56XX' classes. The class was also used on the FP4 Pilot, as mentioned earlier. No. 298 finished her days at Barry shed, and was condemned at Swindon in July 1948.

'1854' class 0–6–0PT No. 906 in Swindon Concentration Yard during the spring of 1948. Built in May 1895, this engine had been allocated to sheds in South Wales ranging from Severn Tunnel Jct. to Fishguard since 1900, and probably before that, too. From 1925, she was predominantly at Neath, and was withdrawn on transfer to Swindon in April 1948. Before the Great War, she spent much time at Swansea Docks, and was doubtless used for shunting and trip duties. From Neath, No.906 was recorded as the Felin Fran Pilot – banking and shunting duties – in October 1936, and probably carried out the same sort of duties towards the end.

'28XX' 2–8–0 No. 3841 passing between Rodbourne Lane box and the engine reception shed outside 'A' shop with an up 'J' class goods in June 1949. The engine was shedded at Reading, and the train may have been one of the Severn Tunnel Jct. to Moreton Cutting services.

No. 2267 was at Swindon Works for a Heavy General repair from late July until early September 1949, and is seen here at the end of that period in the turntable yard between 'A' Shop and the Iron Foundry. The engine is seen coupled to 4,000-gallon 'ROD' tender (No. 2504), with which she ran until July 1950 when her previous tender (3,000-gallon No. 1563) was re-attached at her home shed, Taunton. She was fitted with the Whitaker staff apparatus for use over the Barnstaple and Minehead branches, and was also recorded around this time with spark arrester plates, perhaps for trips into Blinkhorn Depot. The usual spot for the placement of the shed code, on the footplate valance near the bufferbeam, was unavailable due to pipework, so the code 'TN' has been placed on the step between the leading and centre driving wheels.

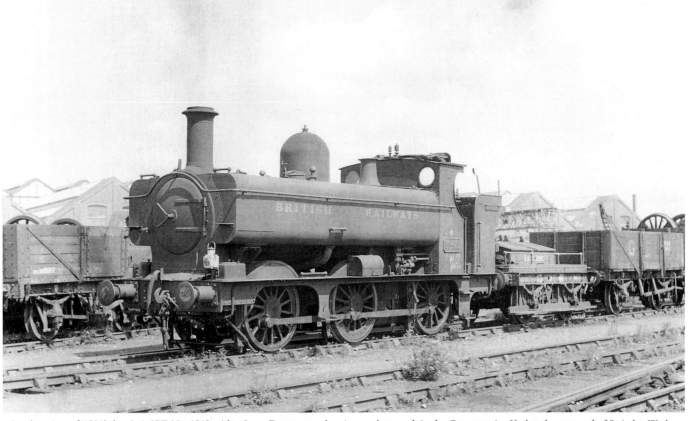

Another view of '1501' class 0–6–0PT No. 1542 with a Loco Department shunting truck at work in the Concentration Yard at the west end of Swindon Works, c.1948. Built in 1880, she was one of five of the class still in service during 1948, but by the end of 1949 she was alone. The earlier '645' series of the class had gone by 1937. No. 1542 was condemned in February 1951.

The Swansea Harbour Trust was vested in the Great Western by an Act of 18th July 1923, in which the company's 14 small locomotives were transferred into GWR stock. These were all 0–4–0 and 0–6–0 saddle tanks, and built by a variety of contractors; Peckett & Sons built SHT 0–6–0ST No. 16 in 1913, and at the grouping this was renumbered 1086. During the Great Western and BR (W) eras, she worked the docks from Danygraig shed, and was renumbered again on 16th March 1949 at Swindon, to 1147. Here, No. 1147 is pictured shunting at Swindon in 1949. She was withdrawn in April 1951.

Swindon 'Saint' No. 2947 *Madresfield Court* leaving Swindon Junction with an up express in 1949. At this time, No. 2947 was a particularly common sight on the 7.50 a.m. Taunton to Paddington, due out of Swindon at 10.53 a.m., which was scheduled to convey a five-coach portion from Cheltenham at the head, then a six-coach section from Taunton, and a Brake Compo from Bristol at the rear. This may have been the service pictured here, making calls at Didcot and Reading en route.

Gloucester housed a pair of 'Saints' (Nos. 2938 and 2951) in 1949, mainly for secondary and relief expresses, local passenger services, and the odd freight working, for the most part over the Swindon and Cardiff routes. On Monday, 21st March 1949, No. 2951 *Tawstock Court* was called upon to work the 3.45 p.m. Carmarthen to Paddington onwards from Cardiff, running non-stop from Newport, and was reported to have carried out the work in the very best tradition of the class. Latterly, she was employed on station pilot duties at Gloucester, and was withdrawn in June 1952. Here, she is seen against the backdrop of the CME's office block at Swindon in 1949.

The other Gloucester 'Saint', No. 2938 *Corsham Court*, seen in the triangle against the CME's offices at Swindon Works in the late 1940s. She moved from Hereford to Gloucester in December 1945, where she was seen on similar duties to No. 2951, again being recorded as the Gloucester station pilot in April 1951. She reappeared at Hereford in early 1952, and was seen on relief trains over the North & West, and London portions of West Midland expresses to and from Worcester. No. 2938 was condemned in August 1952.

By December 1948, only four of the '26XX' class 2–6–0s remained in traffic, based at Stourbridge (2), Gloucester and Pontypool Road. Here, Stourbridge No. 2620 was pictured on Swindon Works triangle in August 1949, now the penultimate engine, condemned, with only 2667 out in traffic. The Stourbridge engines were still hard at work in their final months, being regularly employed on an overnight trip to Bordesley, as well as duties further afield.

Severn Tunnel Jct. '28XX' No. 2815 at Swindon Works triangle in late August 1949, in for a Heavy General repair. Whilst her allocation found her on goods trains to such destinations as Llandilo Jct. (Llanelly), Tavistock Jct. (Plymouth), Weymouth, Salisbury, the London area, and Yarnton (Oxford), she was occasionally utilised on other sheds' turns, and was recorded on the 11.30 p.m. Taunton to Oxley Sdgs, and the 10.0 a.m. Banbury to Newton Abbot.

Cardiff East Dock '2021' class No. 2141 at Swindon Works in 1949. During 1947, she had been on loan to the National Coal Board at Treorchy, though she was back on her normal turns by July 1948, being recorded then at Newtown East Goods Road duty, releasing train engines. She was condemned in October 1950.

Ex-Cardiff Railway 0–6–2T No. 155 leaving Swindon on the Down Gloucester Main with the 3.32 p.m. Swindon to Gloucester pickup goods in the early summer of 1949, passing the stock shed and approaching the Works' Gas Plant. In the distance can be seen the Locomotive Yard signal box, with the bulk of the shed coal stage towering to its left. The engine now carried a copper-capped chimney, and was probably running-in on this duty.

Gloucester 'Saint' No. 2951 *Tavistock Court* on Fairwood troughs, to the west of Westbury, on the evening of Saturday, 23rd July 1949. The train was a down express, but did not carry a reporting number on this busy day, so it may have been the 6.0 p.m. Paddington to Weymouth, which was due out of Westbury at around 8.30 p.m.

A 'Star' with an up express from the West Country taking water on Fairwood troughs in the evening of 23rd July 1949. The setting sun was highlighting the engine's cab, but the near side of the train was in shade. Fairwood troughs, opened in October 1902, were slightly different in length, with the up trough being 495 yards, and the down 553.

The trough refilling after the passage of the express, with wavelets formed by the inrush of water from the storage tank.

Old Oak shed's Brown Boveri gas turbine No. 18000 approaching Swindon with an up express in 1951. At this time, the engine was scheduled for Old Oak Turn No. 1, which came off shed at 6.55 a.m. to work the 7.30 a.m. Paddington to Bristol; the 9.7 a.m. Exeter from Bristol (12.0 noon) to Paddington; the 6.35 p.m. Paddington to Cheltenham as far as Swindon; and the 3.50 p.m. Whitland to Kensington milk, from Swindon (10.5 p.m.) to Southall, thence light to Old Oak Common, due 12.5 a.m. In this view, the engine was probably at the head of the 9.7 a.m. Exeter, which was due to call at Swindon from 1.8 to 1.13 p.m., and would be routed onto the up platform line shortly after passing over the Gloucester line junction, a few yards ahead.

No. 18000 on a less auspicious occasion, being hauled into Temple Meads station by No. 3663 after failing at St. Anne's Park probably with the 7.30 a.m. Paddington in May 1952.

Bath Road shed in the summer of 1952, with Westbury '45XX' No. 4510 in the foreground, and No. 4056 *Princess Margaret* behind. Westbury had local passenger duties to Bristol via Radstock, Wells or Bath, utilising 'Halls', '43XXs' and '45XXs'; there were a total of four '45' duties at this time, one of which ran to Temple Meads (via Radstock), empty stock from Westbury.

Reading 'Hall' No. 5956 *Horsley Hall* assisting a 'Britannia' on a down Welsh express, near Old Oak in 1958, probably working its way home. Cardiff Canton shed worked three 'Britannias' up to London each morning, returning with the 1.55, 3.55 and 5.55 p.m. trains to West Wales. Of these, only the 1.55 p.m. Paddington called at Reading, and this was probably the service seen here. Old Oak West box may be seen near the back of the train.

No. 5974 *Wallsworth Hall* from Westbury shed on a down semi-fast near Kensal Green in 1953, with a '43XX' behind. The train is believed to have been the 5.20 p.m. Paddington to Reading service, on which the Westbury 'Hall' off the 11.40 a.m. Weymouth express (Westbury No. 1 turn) was attached. From Reading, the engine ran light to Newbury, working the 7.18 p.m. thence to Trowbridge; this train comprised the rear part of the 6.0 p.m. Paddington to Weymouth, detached at Newbury.

Against the backdrop of Kensal Green gasholders, a 'King' class 4–6–0 with the 6.30 p.m. Paddington to Weston-super-Mare is seen approaching Old Oak, c. 1954. This was Old Oak Turn No. 1, on which the 'King' worked the 2.25 a.m. Paddington News down to Bristol, the 7.0 am. Weston back from Temple Meads, then the 6.30 p.m. Paddington as far as Bristol, and the 4.9 p.m. Crewe train thence to Plymouth. It brought the 8.0 a.m. Penzance from North Road to Paddington the following day.

Hawksworth '15XX' class 0–6–0PT No. 1504 at Old Oak on empty stock working c. 1962, this duty being Pilot No.6. There were around 22 pilots on weekdays at this time, with a dozen on Sundays, each making between four and twelve movements either inwards to Paddington for departures, or outwards to West London or Old Oak with stock of arrivals. The '15XX' class had just seven locomotives remaining in traffic by this time, five of which were at Old Oak.

A '94XX' class 0–6–0PT approaching Old Oak sidings with an empty stock train in the late 1950s. Nearly all the empty trains ran from or to Old Oak, with West London only supplying around a dozen semi-fast, local and parcels trains.

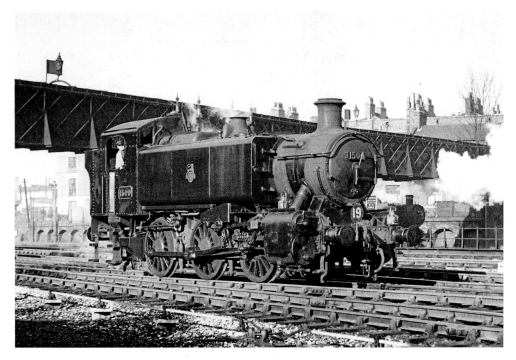

'15XX' class No. 1500 near Royal Oak in 1959. Built in 1949, the ten engines of this class had been divided between the London (6) and Newport Divisions (4) by 1950; at Old Oak, their duties were primarily on the Carriage Pilots. The first withdrawal came in August 1959, after less than ten years' service, with two more in January 1961, and all had gone by the end of 1963.

Alan Clothier is pictured with ROD 2–8–0 No. 3041 at Swindon Stock Shed c.1948. After a short period of storage in 1948, the engine returned to St. Philip's Marsh until September 1953, when she moved to Shrewsbury. The last move in traffic was to Carmarthen, during 1955, where, by the end of 1956, all six remaining engines of the class were gathered. No. 3041 remained in traffic until March 1958.